POSITIVE VIBES ONLY

30 days of prayer and affirmation

By

TERESA B. HOWELL

Copyright © 2018

TeresabHowell.com

Independent Self-Published through Walking In Victory Int. L.L.C

P.O. Box 15171

Durham, NC 27704

Printed in the USA

ISBN: 978-0-9977732-5-5

DEDICATION

This book is dedicated to my Grandmother Era B. Ellis and my mother Helen J. Ellis who both were the apple of my eye. I miss and love you both, R.I.P.

Thinking Positive   Day 1

*Finally, brothers and sisters, whatever is true, whatever is noble, whatever is right, whatever is pure, whatever is lovely, whatever is admirable—if anything is excellent or praiseworthy—think about such things. **Philippians 4:8***

We stagger through our existence with the attempt of peeling away the bad layers of our being. As we get closer to Christ, the bad things that adorn our hearts eventually wash away. We birth new visions, new dreams, and new beginnings after every transformation. But unfortunately, negativity will sometimes creep back into our thought process, tunneling back to us by way of sorrow and pain. All of the positivity that we worked so hard to sustain vanishes and the process starts all over again.

While living in a day of false prophets, diminished ministries, and evil-minded thinkers, we need to invest in nurturing a continuous positive mindset. We don't have to settle for the pain and sorrow, nor should we allow the troubles of this world to keep us down. We also shouldn't allow impoverished views of others to consume us, thus repeating a cycle of lost hope and decreased expectations. The tragedies and hardships around us shouldn't take us backwards. We have to remember God's promises and not settle for mediocre thinking.

Let us build ourselves back up, restock, and regroup knowing that God is with us. The Bible says if any man's work abide which he hath built, he shall receive a reward (*1Corinthians 3:14*). We should work hard in releasing everything that hinders us and allow God in to do the rest.

God will restore a fallen house, repair its damaged walls and restore it to its former glory (*Amos 9:11*). Let Him restore your house today. Turn your sadness into joy, your doubt into hope, and your pain into healing by thinking positive.

He saved us, so that we could have life more abundantly.

Analyze your state of mind. Can you hear, think, and see positively?

If *God* was able to bring us out on yesterday, He can surely bring us out today. So, remain positive and watch God do the rest!

Day 1 Prayer:

Dear Heavenly Father,

Today, I will attempt to keep a positive mindset. No matter what goes on around me, I look to you which cometh my help. Each step I take with you, I learn to walk in your footsteps of positivity. I exalt your name while I walk down this path, to help myself as well as others. It is you that will receive all the honor and the glory. I may stumble and sometimes fall, but I will get back up and try again. Thank you for giving me a changed and positive thought process. Thank you for allowing my light to shine on others. Thank you for your grace and mercy that keeps me moving forward day by day. I praise you and I honor you. I worship and adore you. I give you thanks for all of my many blessings...

In Jesus Name,

Amen

Life is like a game of chess. To win you have to make positive moves.

Allen Rufus

Today's Affirmation:

_____

_____

_____

_____

_____

_____

_____

Positive Words:

_____

_____

_____

_____

_____

_____

_____

Journal your thoughts:

_____

_____

_____

_____

_____

_____

*Since, then, you have been raised with Christ, set your hearts on things above, where Christ is, seated at the right hand of God. Set your minds on things above, not on earthly things. - **Colossians 3:1-2***

Does God reign in every section of your heart?

It's challenging for most to give a firm "yes," but all things are possible. We have so many daily obstacles that steer us away from our Godly focus. The enemy is busy, trying to lull us into a state of disbelief, in order to disconnect our hearts from God's will and purpose.

Recently in the news, there were several students killed in a Florida high school. As an educator, it broke my heart and I sulked for days, going into deep prayer for the students and their families. But, after a week of analyzation, I realized that the sadness of the event had consumed me. It left me afraid of moving forward in education and I found myself looking for another career. Eventually, I had to separate myself from the pain and affliction in order to produce a harvest of righteousness and peace (**Hebrews 12:11**). Satan was trying his best to kill, steal, and destroy every level of normalcy for education. But the Bible says in (**2 Corinthians 12:9a)** that our strength is made perfect in our weakness. Instead of losing hope and allowing the adversary to pull at my heart strings, I fought back and allowed my hurting heart to remain in the hands of the Father.

A few days later, the news reported that several students took a stand to end the shootings in schools. A large crowd gathered in Washington, D.C., making a plea for the government to create gun laws that would protect us from this kind of mayhem. They gave birth to a new mindset and their hearts were strengthened to move forward with peace and love, in spite of the forsaken tragedy. The scripture says that His power will rest upon us. Do you believe that? It did with those group of students that took a stand. It can rest in us as well.

I encourage you to practice on setting your heart on things above. His presence will calm troubled spirits, ease the pain of our losses, and eventually allow positive vibes to flow within a broken heart.

Let positive vibes sync into your heart today. The thought alone should have your heart leaping about the goodness of Jesus. Remember to do your heart exercises daily with a good scripture, prayer, or positive quote.

Day 2 Prayer:

Father God,

Allow your joy to shine through my heart.   I know that you are in the middle of it all and you will take care of your people. Please cover our hearts and clear our minds.

In Jesus Name,

Amen

"Be still and know that I am God...Wait on the Lord and be of good courage. Guard your heart above all else, for it is the source of life."

You change your life by changing your heart.

Max Lucado

Today's Affirmation:

_____

_____

_____

_____

_____

_____

_____

Positive Words:

_____

_____

_____

_____

_____

_____

_____

Journal your thoughts:

_____

_____

_____

_____

_____

_____

_____

Speak Positively   Day 3

*May these words of my mouth and this meditation of my heart be pleasing in your sight, Lord, my Rock and my Redeemer. - **Psalm 19:14***

Positive words have a great influence on positive outcomes. I'm sure you heard the scripture, *life and death is in the power of the tongue.* I'm a living witness…it's true! It's almost like painting a picture. I start off with a clean canvas and a colorful backdrop. I would say to myself, I *will* create a masterpiece. I spoke something positive into the atmosphere and I believed that the goal would be accomplished. I programmed my mind not to settle for a mediocre painting. I put my trust in God with determination to create a magnificent final product. My words turned into action and my actions turned into reality. Throughout the painting process, I cultivated that masterpiece through faith.   Meanwhile, the Holy Spirit led me into the direction that I wanted to go and gave me the power to make that perfect picture.

"As we know all things work together for the good to them that love God, to them who are called according to His purpose."

Maybe my first try didn't turn out the way I planned. But, I continued to speak it, believe it, and found a great sense of purpose while painting my masterpiece.

That's what *positive* words can do for all of us. If we keep speaking it, God will excel our gifts and give us great power to complete the mission. What we want to achieve can eventually come to pass, because we held on to our *faith*.

Being an author, I was determined to be a success in the literary world. I only spoke positively about my writing, because I knew that God had given me the gift of storytelling. By the time my third novel came out, I shocked myself with a new level of writing skills. I believed it, I received it, and I thanked God for it. My practice was made perfect. God perfected my gift and my *"masterpiece"* was complete.

Your words are powerful. It can determine the success and failure of your masterpiece. When you speak life, obtain it. Positive words will help you align your purpose with God's plan. I encourage you to SPEAK LIFE into your situation and that can only be done by speaking positive. Learn to have unshakeable faith in all that you do!

Day 3 Prayer:

Father God,

I ask as it says in Psalms 141:3 to set a guard over my mouth and keep a watch over the door of my lips. Allow my positive words to touch the hearts of many so that they can see the God in me. Father, I asked that you give me the words to say and the instructions on how to use them positively. I know my words can affect myself and others. For I am learning my purpose and I know that by speaking positive and powerful words, all things are possible. Only you have the power to transform things that I cannot see into visual proof of your goodness. I know it starts with my faith and how I believe. For you are worthy of all the glory and all the praise. It's in your precious name I pray.

In Jesus Name,

Amen

Your words become your world.

Nadeem Kazi

Today's Affirmation:

_____
_____
_____
_____
_____
_____
_____

Positive Words:

_____
_____
_____
_____
_____
_____

Journal your thoughts:

_____
_____
_____
_____
_____
_____

A Positive Praise   Day 4

Rejoice always, pray continually, give thanks in all circumstances; for this is God's will for you in Christ Jesus. Do not quench the Spirit. **1 Thessalonians 5:16-19**

Now that you have positive vibes flowing through your mind, heart and soul…let's praise Him!

Rejoice in the Lord. Again, I say rejoice!

Continuously give thanks for everything that God has provided in your life. Didn't He give you a sound and changed mind? Didn't He give you a clean heart? Didn't He give you a renewed spirit? If He hasn't, you still have time to obtain all of those things and more. Let's keep the joy of the Lord as our strength and move past any negativity that may come our way. For He is King of Kings and Lord of Lords.

David danced despite everything he had gone through. He felt he owed it to God and rejoiced through his pain.

Day 4 Prayer:

Father God,

Lord, I praise you right where I stand for each and every day that I have a pulse. I have limbs to walk, eyes to see, and ears to hear and I thank you. Where would I be without you? I praise you for being my healer, keeper, helper, strength, redeemer, way maker, provider, and mighty strong tower. No one compares to the love you give and I long to be closer to you. With my whole heart on this day, I praise you.

In Jesus Name,

Amen

From the rising of the sun to the place where it sets, the name of the Lord is to be praised.

Psalm 113: 2-4

Today's Affirmation:

_____

_____

_____

_____

_____

_____

Positive Words:

_____

_____

_____

_____

_____

_____

Journal your thoughts:

_____

_____

_____

_____

_____

_____

Positive Prayers   Day 5

*And pray in the Spirit on all occasions with all kinds of prayers and requests. With this in mind, be alert and always keep on praying for all the Lord's people. - **Ephesians 6:18***

Prayer is the main ingredient to a balanced spiritual meal. Our prayers don't have to be long and deep to get into God's ears. The one-word prayer that will always be effective is calling on the name of JESUS. Calling on His name in the midnight hour can be just enough prayer to ease your spirit when you don't know what else to say.

Did you know that God hears every prayer rendered?

David said in (**Psalm 116:1**): *I love the LORD because he hears my voice and my prayer for mercy. Because he bends down to listen, I will pray as long as I have breath!*

Prayer changes things. Try it and watch God move on your behalf!

Day 5 Prayer:

Father God,

Let nothing separate me from you. Help me to walk in the right direction as I know great is your love towards me. Help me to remember that you hear every prayer and you will answer when it is time. I strive for patience as I wait on you while being of good faith and courage.

In Jesus Name,

Amen

We have to pray with our eyes on God, not on the difficulties.

Oswald Chambers

Today's Affirmation:

_____

_____

_____

_____

_____

_____

Positive Words:

_____

_____

_____

_____

_____

_____

Journal your thoughts:

_____

_____

_____

_____

_____

_____

*My son do not forget my teaching, but keep my commands in your heart, for they will prolong your life many years and bring you peace and prosperity. Let love and faithfulness never leave you; bind them around your neck, write them on the tablet of your heart. Then you will win favor and a good name in the sight of God and man. - **Proverbs 3:1-4***

God teaches us to love one another as we love ourselves. Without love where would we be? Yes, I know what you're thinking...some people make it difficult to love them, right? Yes, certain people can truly clog up our arteries with deception, whining, and immaturity...the list goes on. But, guess what? There will always be that particular person considered the thorn in your side, no matter how much you love them. That's one of the obstacles that comes with trying to love. We have to love everyone in spite of their faults and even when it's not reciprocatcd.

Paul attempted to maintain heretics and later became the greatest missionary to ever live in biblical times. He didn't give up and he didn't let the actions of others stop him from loving people or loving God. He wrote letters to several groups of individuals, because they errored in the faith. But, Paul didn't stop his mission. He knew it was going to be a work in progress, especially for the individuals that didn't have a clean heart.

Let's face the facts. We are all on different levels when it comes to love, forgiveness, and salvation. You may not always "like" everyone that you meet, but the Bible says in spite of it all, we must love them.

I know, I know…Sister So and So works your nerves every Sunday. And Brother Talkative makes your skin crawl to the utmost. But, you are on an assignment, just like apostle Paul. God will preserve you as chains are broken when dealing with difficult personalities.

Do you realize how many times God has intervened when I felt like giving up on my sister or brother? He had to, because if He didn't, there would be a lot of physical altercations and massive fallouts amongst God's people. God had me covered!

Let your new name be *transformer,* because if God didn't transform our hate into love…where would we be?

Display positive love…to ***everyone***.

Day 6 Prayer:

Dear Heavenly Father,

Teach me how to love even my enemies. I want your love to shine brightly for all to see. I ask that you give my heart the desire to love unconditionally. I want my love to be infectious and travel near and far. I want my love to change lives and allow people to see only you. Show me how to love, even when I don't want to.

In Jesus Name,

Amen

When the power of love overcomes the love of power, the world will know peace.

Jimi Hendrix

Today's Affirmation:

_____

_____

_____

_____

_____

_____

_____

Positive Words:

_____

_____

_____

_____

_____

_____

_____

Journal your thoughts:

_____

_____

_____

_____

_____

_____

_____

Positive Actions   Day 7

*For God has not given us a spirit of fear, but of power and of love and of a sound mind. **2 Timothy 1:7***

Positive actions can cause a domino effect, especially in a room full of people. Most people thrive off of positive energy. Do you remember those Michael Jackson concerts shown on prime-time television? When he would start to dance, everyone around him would join in. He had this positive energy that made people forget about what they were going through and they mimicked all of his actions.

Don't you want to have that kind of energy or power to change the world? It all starts with positive actions. Michael Jackson had everyone trying to moonwalk across the floor. Even women in high heels would take the chance, with an attempt to do it just like he did. So, don't be fearful of what the world thinks. Commit a positive action for yourself, for your community, or even for your church. You never know, that one positive trend might help someone forget about their troubles on a rainy day.

It doesn't take much to display a positive action. Whether it's giving a smile to someone that wears a frown or buying a coworker a *just because* lunch…Positive actions can change negative energy instantly. You will notice the people around changing after they follow your lead. Just like they did the infamous, Michael Jackson.

Remember: God was denied and ridiculed by many. But, it never stopped Him from displaying positive actions to the masses. He never gave up nor did he give in to negative energy around Him.

He rose from the dead, so we might live again…the ultimate positive action.

Day 7 Prayer:

Father God,

Lord, I want to imitate your ways and be more like you. Allow my daily actions to shine. Allow my light to glow amongst your people. Give me the power to help others forget about their troubles are smile when they are feeling low. Give me the ultimate positive action to be an agent of change wherever I go.

In Jesus Name,

Amen

You can spread positivity by creating something positive, or by reflecting positively in your thoughts and actions.

Anil Sinha

Today's Affirmation:

_____

_____

_____

_____

_____

_____

_____

Positive Words:

_____

_____

_____

_____

_____

_____

Journal your thoughts:

_____

_____

_____

_____

_____

_____

Positive Commitment   Day 8

Commit your actions to the LORD, and your plans will succeed.
Proverbs 16:3

Do you remember the day you decided to follow Christ?

What a positive commitment to change your lifestyle and be a living witness for the one that died for our sins. It was simple, right? All you did was confess with your mouth that you believed in He who is Lord. With this confession you were promised everlasting life. Jesus offers us a right to commit to Him. He doesn't force us. He gives us a choice.

The commitment, however, can sometimes fall short as we are made of flesh and will sometimes stumble. Paul said he had to die daily. He was referencing his flesh and how it was a daily walk with God. The same thing applies to us as well. But, guess what? No matter how many times we fall short of our commitment, God still takes us back with opened arms when we repent. He doesn't punish us for giving up on Him. He accepts us back without question. Even when we feel we don't deserve his love, He gives it to us anyway.

If you haven't committed…try Him.

If you're unsure…trust Him.

*Therefore, I urge you, brethren, by the mercies of God, to present your bodies a living and holy sacrifice, acceptable to God, which is your spiritual service of worship. And do not be conformed to this world, but be transformed by the renewing of your mind, so that you may prove what the will of God is, that which is good and acceptable and perfect. (**Romans 12: 1-2**)*

When you commit to Him wholeheartedly, you WIN.

Day 8 Prayer:

Father God,

You gave your only begotten son so that I may not perish. With this in mind, I present a covenant to your Holy name that I will give you all the praise and all the honor for the rest of my days. God, lead me to the path of righteousness and order my steps in the direction of which you would have me to go.

In Jesus Name,

Amen

Commitment is what transforms a promise into reality.

Abraham Lincoln

Today's Affirmation:

_____

_____

_____

_____

_____

_____

Positive Words:

_____

_____

_____

_____

_____

_____

Journal your thoughts:

_____

_____

_____

_____

_____

_____

Positive Light   Day 9

Do all things without grumbling or questioning, that you may be blameless and innocent, children of God without blemish in the midst of a crooked and twisted generation, among whom you shine as lights in the world. - **Philippians 2:14-15**

You can have all the positive words and scriptures in the world in front of you. But, if you have a bad attitude, your light will become dim to the people around you. You now have several gateways, such as your new heart, your new mind, and your new spirit to formulate that positive attitude that the world needs.

So, I'm sure you have asked the question: why is it that some people stay the same even after making the proclamation of following Christ and creating a positive light? There will always be individuals who will state that they want to be like Christ, but in their minds, certain scriptures they read don't always apply to them and the world they live in.

"Make a tree good and its fruit will be good or make a tree bad and its fruit will be bad, for a tree is recognized by its fruit." **(Matthew 12:33)**

Be recognized by good fruit and let the bad attitude depart from your spirit. The people of today need unconditional love, not attitude. The world is withering away, and we don't have time to waste with bad disposition and dimmed lights.

A Samaritan woman at the well didn't really know herself. But, one thing was for sure, she knew Jews didn't like Samaritans and they displayed bad attitudes. Jesus came along asking for a drink. The woman was very surprised because his attitude was different from other Jews that she had come across. He talked to her, gave her kind words, even spoke into her life. She went back and told the other Samaritans about this Jew that was kind and proclaimed to be the Messiah. She said, "Come and meet a man who told me everything I ever did!" This Samaritan woman assisted with the connection of two groups of people who didn't get along due to beliefs, misconceptions, and bad attitudes (*John 4: 1-54*). Jesus came along, shined his positive light, and a village of Samaritans believed that He was indeed the Savior of the world.

Model and amplify a positive light today for all of the world to see.

Day 9 Prayer:

Father God,

Formulate my positive gateways of light for all of the world to see. Mold me into whom you would like for me to be. I want to present good fruit and be recognized as one of your children. Remove the blemishes and create a glow that will be pleasing in your sight.

In Jesus Name,

Amen

> **When you let your light shine, you unconsciously give others permission to do the same.**
>
> **Nelson Mandela**

Today's Affirmation:

_____

_____

_____

_____

_____

_____

_____

Positive Words:

_____

_____

_____

_____

_____

_____

_____

Journal your thoughts:

_____

_____

_____

_____

_____

_____

_____

Do you not know? Have you not heard? The LORD is the everlasting God, the Creator of the ends of the earth. He will not grow tired or weary, and his understanding no one can fathom. He gives strength to the weary and increases the power of the weak. Even youths grow tired and weary, and young men stumble and fall; but those who hope in the LORD will renew their strength. They will soar on wings like eagles; they will run and not grow weary, they will walk and not be faint. **Isaiah 40:28-31**

Did you wake up this morning feeling motivated?

Have the troubles of this world pushed your motivation down to your feet? I know that feeling well. This thing called life can truly beat you up and pounce all over the little motivation you have left to give.

But, guess what? After reading the Bible verse for day 10 of this series, I was motivated to conquer the world and I hope you will too! Just knowing that God understands us, He hears our cry, and He will not allow us to stumble or fall. Knowing that just gave me all the motivation I needed for today. Renew your strength in Him and watch everything fall into place. Thus, causing an abundance of motivation. He is an everlasting God that will never let you down.

Day 10 Prayer:

Father God,

I am motivated by your power and your mercy. I aim to be diligent and stay motivated to push through every negative situation. Strengthen me, oh Lord, as my intentions are pure and true.

In Jesus Name,

Amen

People often say that motivation doesn't last. Well neither does bathing, that's why we recommend it daily.

Zig Ziglar

Today's Affirmation:

_____

_____

_____

_____

_____

_____

_____

Positive Words:

_____

_____

_____

_____

_____

_____

_____

Journal your thoughts:

_____

_____

_____

_____

_____

_____

_____

But you are a chosen race, a royal priesthood, a holy nation, a people for his own possession, that you may proclaim the excellencies of him who called you out of darkness into his marvelous light. **1 Peter 2:9**

Do you really believe that everyone has a positive self-image?

You are altogether beautiful, my love; there is no flaw in you.

(Songs of Solomon 4:7)

There it is right there…right in his word. You are altogether beautiful, and you should know this because you are a child of God. Knowing that you are part of His royal family should make you beam from ear to ear. You should never think negative of yourself because you are part of the ultimate kingdom. If you don't feel pretty enough, don't feel smart enough, or not feeling strong enough, you must remember where you come from. That alone should boost your esteem.

Look in the mirror and repeat these words, "I am fearfully and wonderfully made." Don't forget that!

God created man in his own image, in the image of God he created him; male and female he created them. Psalm 1:27

Day 11 Prayer:

Father God,

I am beautiful because you made me this way. I am powerful because you made me this way. I am wiser because you made me this way. I am a conqueror because you made me this way! The closer I walk with you, the more I can see my own self-image blossom. I am grateful for how you created me.

In Jesus Name,

Amen

A positive self-image is the best possible preparation for success in life.

Dr. Joyce Brothers

Today's Affirmation:

_____

_____

_____

_____

_____

_____

_____

Positive Words:

_____

_____

_____

_____

_____

_____

Journal your thoughts:

_____

_____

_____

_____

_____

_____

Blessed is the man who walks not in the counsel of the wicked, nor stands in the way of sinners, nor sits in the seat of scoffers; but his delight is in the law of the LORD, and on his law, he meditates day and night. He is like a tree planted by streams of water that yields its fruit in its season, and its leaf does not wither. In all that he does, he prospers. The wicked are not so but are like chaff that the wind drives away. Therefore, the wicked will not stand in the judgment, nor sinners in the congregation of the righteous; **Psalms 1:1-6**

Have you ever found yourself seeking counsel from someone who doesn't have it all together? They are probably worst off than you are but, you sit and listen attentively as if they are telling you something profound. I have. After I received the advice, I was more messed up when I left out, than before I came in. What I didn't realize was sometimes you have people who don't want to see you succeed, so their advice might be a little biased.

We have those amongst us who stay close by in the wings of our green room to destroy God's plan for our lives. It's a sad commentary, but it happens to the best of us.

Remember, there are some things that God will do for us that is solely for us. It can't be duplicated nor shared with your friends and family. That's just the way it is. Your blessings are just that: YOUR blessings. We can't always take advice from others just because they claim to be the expert in OUR situation. When we walk into this form of negativity, go to God. The truth is, we probably should've gone to HIM in the first place. Don't share information with the sneaky, jealous people that have walked in your green room and tend to linger onto your stage of life, instead of their own. *Your* stage belongs to who God created it for…YOU!

A friend of mine once said that God shows up late at night when everyone is asleep for a reason. You know why? Because He knows that is the time when our minds are settled, and we have the least amount of distractions, which include other people. Pay attention to the people around you and the counsel that you receive. When you can't find a human relationship that is desirable, go to the most positive counselor

of them all, Jesus! He will be all the positive counsel you need.

Day 12 Prayer:

Father God,

My ears are open and ready to hear from you. I seek your counsel and guidance. If I am approached by a human vessel, let the words from their mouth come straight from you. Give me the gift to discern who is for me and who is against me. Give me the insight to see through the fog of my enemies. Put me in good company of people that will love me and have my best interest at heart.

In Jesus Name,

Amen

Gods advice is like a proverb: the meaning depends on the interpretation.

Rebecca L. Walkowitz

Today's Affirmation:

_____

_____

_____

_____

_____

_____

_____

Positive Words:

_____

_____

_____

_____

_____

_____

Journal your thoughts:

_____

_____

_____

_____

_____

_____

_____

Positive Planning   Day 13

Trust in the LORD with all your heart, and do not lean on your own understanding. In all your ways acknowledge him, and he will make straight your path- **Proverbs 3:5-6**

Planning without God in the midst might be problematic for some. In 2016, I planned to be a phenomenal writer someday. But, I didn't pray about it, nor did I seek God on how to start the process. Wrong move...

In my mind, I had it all mapped out. I went around in circles, trying to figure out the process, when all I had to was listen to God's instruction. The lesson I learned: never go into planning without Jesus leading the way. He is the author and finisher of it all.

God told the Virgin Mary what He had planned for her life. Mary questioned the possibilities (*Luke 1:34*). She was thinking only in the natural and was used to babies being created with help from a man. But, God had a plan. God explained to Mary that the Holy Spirit was going to do the work. In other words, the Master had the plan in his hands. Just as God was creative in bringing forth new life, He can also be creative with the plan He has for YOU. We have to follow His plan and when we do, it becomes a smooth ride on this rocky roller coaster we call life. *For I know the plans I have for you, declares the LORD, plans for welfare and not for evil, to give you a future and a hope.* **(Jeramiah 29:11)**

Day 13 Prayer:

Father God,

I humble myself to thee. I give you all the honor and the praise. You have the complete blueprint of my life and I come to you first, while planning each level of my life.

In Jesus Name,

Amen

God wrecks your plans, when he sees that your plans are about to wreck you.

The Soul Doctor

Today's Affirmation:

_____

_____

_____

_____

_____

_____

_____

Positive Words:

_____

_____

_____

_____

_____

_____

_____

Journal your thoughts:

_____

_____

_____

_____

_____

_____

_____

Positive Expectations   Day 14

My soul wait thou only upon God; for my expectation [is] from him.
– Psalm 62:5

God asked Joshua to be strong and courageous, because He was always with him. Joshua commanded the officers of Israel to get ready for the new provisions of crossing the Jordan River, and taking possession of the land that the Lord gave to him. He had high expectations, because he knew without a shadow of a doubt, that the Lord was on his side. Just as God prepared Joshua for his next move, He can prepare you too. God tells us that He will never abandon us, and He keeps his promises.

So, with that in mind, I have high expectations that God will see me through all challenges and obstacles that come my way. (*Joshua 1:8*) states to meditate everything written in His word day and night. By giving God some of our time, God has promised a full and satisfying life. God had Joshua's back and He has yours too. Have positive expectations that He will see you through. *But my God shall supply all your need according to his riches in glory by Christ Jesus.* (*Philippians 4:19*)

Day 14 Prayer:

Father God,

Lord, I come to you with high expectations. I know you are a keeper of your promises and your word is true. I have high expectations to excel and do great things, because you have my back. I know your power is great and you can move every mountain that stands in my way of my destiny. Show me the way.

In Jesus Name,

Amen

High expectations are the key to everything.

Sam Walton

Today's Affirmation:

_____

_____

_____

_____

_____

_____

Positive Words:

_____

_____

_____

_____

_____

Journal your thoughts:

_____

_____

_____

_____

_____

_____

Accepting Positive Instruction   Day 15

*Listen to advice and accept instruction, that you may gain wisdom in the future. – **Proverbs 19:20***

There was once a time where the younger generation would always listen attentively to the older generation before them. They would sit under a seasoned individual and gain knowledge for success. This was also seen in the old testament of the Bible. God used a woman by the name of Deborah to give instruction to the kings after Joshua's death. Women back then were viewed as second-class citizens, but God used Deborah and Jael to free Israel from oppression by the Canaanites. If God can use Deborah in a mighty way to give positive instruction to others for change, He can use you too. Don't judge a book by its cover. Deborah was one of the most influential judges in the land. She rallied troops against the Canaanite army and Israel was set free. There is someone that might enter your life with positive instruction and just might have the keys to your mental and spiritual freedom. God can use anyone to get the job

done.

Day 15 Prayer:

Father God,

Allow me not to judge individuals that enter into my life with positive instruction. Allow me to have open ears and realize that they were sent by you. Not everyone has ill intent. Let me see the good in people. Let me open up to those that want the best for my life and can instruct me to a positive path.

In Jesus Name,

Amen

Tell me and I forget. Teach me and I remember.
Involve me and I learn.

Benjamin Franklin

Today's Affirmation:

_____

_____

_____

_____

_____

_____

Positive Words:

_____

_____

_____

_____

_____

_____

Journal your thoughts:

_____

_____

_____

_____

_____

_____

Positive Influence   Day 16

Whoever walks with the wise becomes wise, but the companion of fools will suffer harm. – *Proverbs 13:20*

Deborah influenced a lot of people as told in Day 15. Her positive influence resulted to a free Israelite nation. But there was also another influential female in the Bible that reached others. Her name was Ruth. Her story of having a desperate situation of losing her husband and everything she had was significant. Why? Because, despite what she was going through, she surrendered to God.

Her love and loyalty influenced Naomi to stand strong. Naomi was then influenced by their connection, thus turning it around to give Ruth some good advice. Ruth did as Naomi instructed and soon found favor from a businessman named Boaz. By Ruth giving positive influence during her time of trouble, it was reciprocated, and God made a way. Ruth gleaned from his harvest and Boaz took over the debt of Ruth's deceased husband, which led to marriage. Their union continued the lineage of King David to Jesus. One person's pain influenced another to still believe. She surrendered her life to God, pressed her way, and was blessed by God in the end. She persevered and gave a positive influence that changed her situation (*Ruth 4:105*). Reading the book of Ruth was encouraging, as it showed God's faithfulness for His people. I hope her story will do the same for you.

Day 16 Prayer:

Father God,

Allow me to be a positive influence to others that will receive it. Show me how to connect with individuals, even when I am going through tough times. Keep me motivated to witness to others and be that influential spark that will motivate them to seek your face. Help me to lift others, while in a desperate situation like Ruth. Give me the courage to continue a journey of positivity.

In Jesus Name,

Amen

She was a woman of positive influence who was all about progressing. She wanted things to change and grow.

Jessica Brown

Today's Affirmation:

_____

_____

_____

_____

_____

_____

_____

Positive Words:

_____

_____

_____

_____

_____

_____

_____

Journal your thoughts:

_____

_____

_____

_____

_____

_____

_____

Positive Association   Day 17

Do not be misled: "Bad company corrupts good character – 1
Corinthians 15:33

Positive association correlates with positive influences. As the Scripture states, bad company can corrupt our positive character or image. I can remember as early as third grade, when there was a group of girls that were always getting in trouble in class. Instead of moving away from the chaos, I wanted to be right smack dab in the middle of the drama. I realized after getting in trouble several times that my bad company was bringing forth a bad change. I talked differently, I acted differently, and responded to others differently, due to the company I kept around me.

It was as if I stepped into a pile of quicksand and it was hard to stand up tall and be the person that God called me to be. My teacher pulled me aside, letting me know that I didn't belong with this particular group of girls. I was different, and it showed. Being associated with the wrong crowd will always have a negative impact in some form or fashion. It was then after being chastised by my teacher that I realized to seek positive associations that would spark positive vibes in my life. Birds of a feather truly do flock together.

Day 17 Prayer:

Father God,

Give us the tools needed to associate with good and loving individuals. Allow us to see through the good and the bad. We must remain in good character by finding the right group of individuals to associate ourselves with.

In Jesus Name,

Amen

Surround yourself with those on the same mission as you.

Anonymous

Today's Affirmation:

_____

_____

_____

_____

_____

_____

Positive Words:
_____

_____

_____

_____

_____

Journal your thoughts:
_____

_____

_____

_____

_____

_____

Positively Fearless   Day 18

Don't fear, for I have redeemed you; I have called you by name; you are Mine." Isaiah 43:1

How can you fear anything with God on your side? HE will take care of you. Where would we be if fear controlled us day and night? Nothing would get accomplished, no one would win competitions, run for president, or even travel outside of the United States.

 I used to fear flying as a child. Once I became an adult, I realized if it's my time to go, it's God's will. I learned to enjoy life without worrying about things that I cannot control. I left it all in God's hands. Life is much sweeter when you allow God to work out the fear in your life. Never fear, God is always there.

Be strong, do not fear: your God will come, he will come with vengeance; with divine retribution he will come to save you." (Isaiah 35:4)

Day 18 Prayer:

Father God,

I lift my hands up and give it all to you. I trust you and know that you will be my help in a time of trouble. I do not fear the things of this world as I know you are right there with me.

In Jesus Name,

Amen

Whatever you fear most has no power. It is your fear that has the power.

Oprah Winfrey

Today's Affirmation:

_____

_____

_____

_____

_____

_____

_____

Positive Words:

_____

_____

_____

_____

_____

_____

_____

Journal your thoughts:

_____

_____

_____

_____

_____

_____

_____

Positive Works   Day 19

In the same way, let your light shine before others, so that they may see your good works and give glory to your Father who is in heaven. – Matthew 5:16

Your positive works should speak volumes to people around you. But remember, works alone won't get you to heaven. You must have the work, along with a relationship with Christ. Some people show their work all their lives by helping their community, church, and job. But, is there a relationship with Christ that is also attached? Connect the two and watch God bring you to an entirely new level.

For we are his workmanship, created in Christ Jesus for good works, which God prepared beforehand, that we should walk in them. (Ephesians 2:10)

God prepared you…get to know Him…now go to work.

Day 19 Prayer:

Father God,

You have given me the tools that I need to get the work done. It is a gift from you. I will not focus on works alone, but I will also draw closer to you.

In Jesus Name,

Amen

Work is love made visible.

Kahlil Gibran

Today's Affirmation:

_____

_____

_____

_____

_____

_____

Positive Words:

_____

_____

_____

_____

_____

Journal your thoughts:

_____

_____

_____

_____

_____

_____

Conquering with Positivity   Day 20

*Nay, in all these things we are more than conquerors through him that loved us-**Romans 8:37***

My church has a slogan that states, ***Overcomers never quit, and quitters never overcome.***

I dare not quit when I have God on my side. I am more than a conqueror and I trust God's promises. Jesus didn't stop when his disciples turned against Him. He still had passion, even while on the cross (***John 19: 23-24***). His love was exemplified, and He showed us that in spite of the nailed hands, the torture, and the death, He rose again and conquered the world. Being on the cross for our sins didn't shake Him nor move Him. His passion superseded His circumstance.

I get chills down my spine writing about this. Why can't we have that kind of passion to positively conquer our destiny? When you abide in Christ, strengthen your connection, and build your faith…things happen. You are more than a conqueror and you can defeat the enemy in a mighty way with Christ. Trials will come, resurrections will be performed, but Jesus will be right there for you.

Peter wanted to quit during the week of the crucifixion. He failed Jesus in a mighty way. But, when Jesus spoke to him, Peter changed. He began to believe, and he learned how to become a conqueror by accepting God's power. Although he struggled with it, he moved forward. Thus, creating a huge impact in the lives of others. He stumbled, he fell, he got up, he conquered. God will give you the abilities to conquer, even when things don't look possible to do so.

Day 20 Prayer:

Father God,

Thank you for giving me the power and the strength to conquer and win. I bless your name for every time that I've pushed forward, despite the obstacles and challenges before me. I am like Joshua…I expect you to move things out of my way to get to my destiny. I'm a living witness that you will come late in the midnight hour and turn everything around in my favor. I worship you and adore you.

In Jesus Name,

Amen

Life throws challenges and over every challenge comes with rainbows and lights to conquer it.

Amy Ray

Today's Affirmation:

_____
_____
_____
_____
_____
_____
_____

Positive Words:

_____
_____
_____
_____
_____
_____
_____

Journal your thoughts:

_____
_____
_____
_____
_____
_____
_____

Changing Positively   Day 21

See, I am doing a new thing! Now it springs up; do you not perceive it?
I am making a way in the wilderness and streams in the wasteland.
– **Isaiah 43:19**

There is a song that I used to sing in church. The lyrics talked about, "When I looked back over my life...how I truly changed." My testimony is a strong one when dealing with change. I can write another book about trials to triumph...that's truly my story. But, the positive change came when I gave my life to Christ. My tables were completely turned, and my pain was recycled into joy. If you have a strong desire to be changed, you can be cured from the pain and make a positive impact.

In 1992, I was in a car accident that changed my life. I had two broken femurs, a broken ankle, broken fingers, and ripped knees. Even though I wasn't the driver, I thought I would never drive or ride on a highway ever again. I feared riding in the front seat for years and would break down every time I saw a terrible accident on the side of the road. But, I hated that feeling and I desired change. I didn't want to live in fear, so I prayed for God to take it all away. God took that strong desire and renewed my strength. Not only did God renew my desire to drive fearlessly, I now have the courage to drive long distance to other states. I put my trust solely in Him and the change came suddenly.

Day 21 Prayer:

Father God,

Thank you for a changed mindset. You have given me the power to see things in a positive light. You have rearranged my thought process like the Samaritan woman and I feel brand new. I see things clearer and I know that in everything you are there. I praise you, for you've taken the fear away. I honor you for the journey and I am thankful to see a new day in a brand-new way.

In Jesus Name,

Amen

The secret to change is to focus all of your energy not on fighting the old, but on building the new.

Socrates

Today's Affirmation:

_____

_____

_____

_____

_____

_____

_____

Positive Words:

_____

_____

_____

_____

_____

_____

_____

Journal your thoughts:

_____

_____

_____

_____

_____

_____

_____

So, shall My word be which goes forth from My mouth; it shall not return to Me empty, without accomplishing what I desire, and without succeeding in the matter for which I sent it. – Isaiah 55:11

Isaiah was a prophet that gave the people of Judah several warnings about their sins. He told them that God's plan for salvation was going to establish eternal peace. He also talked about the keys needed to open several doors, in order to receive it. He had hope that the people of Israel would trust in the Lord, to find the peace, he spoke of. It was a challenging assignment, but despite the Israelites' self-centered and spoiled ways, he continued to be a positive witness.

Judah become self-reliant and felt they didn't need God in the picture. But, Isaiah kept being a positive witness for God, even when he became discouraged concerning their actions. He was mocked, laughed at, and even accused of being condescending. The people of Judah didn't want to hear all the Godly talk, they wanted to hear nice things that made them feel good about their situation. But, Isaiah was not going to push forth words for God that wasn't the truth. He refused for his words to fall short of what he tried to accomplish.

As shown in the book of Isaiah, positive witnessing became a true challenge for the prophet. But, he was determined to do what was right by telling the people the truth. Sometimes, being a witness, you must tell people what they aren't ready to hear. You must follow God's will to help resolve doubts with the non-believers.

One thing is for sure, even when you don't witness verbally, as a Christian, your life should demonstrate the Good News of Jesus Christ. Isaiah told about God's blessings. They weren't solely for the Israelites. These blessings would be given to all that committed to the Lord. Let not your positive witnessing be given to just a certain group of people. Positive witnessing should be performed to everyone that you meet. Whether it's verbal or nonverbal, God wants to use you.

Isaiah was determined to continue to spread the good news, no matter the reaction. He became a positive witness that attempted to bring hope and peace to Jerusalem. As believers, we should have that same mindset: become a positive witness that will bring hope and peace to our dying nation. God is counting on you!

Day 22 Prayer:

Father God,

Give me the words to say to others about who you are and why you saved us.   Guide my steps each time I talk about your goodness. Let everyone I meet see your light.

In Jesus Name,

Amen

Relax, let go, but remember only one thing: you are a witness.

Osho

Today's Affirmation:

_____
_____
_____
_____
_____
_____
_____

Positive Words:

_____
_____
_____
_____
_____
_____
_____

Journal your thoughts:

_____
_____
_____
_____
_____
_____
_____

Build a large boat from cypress wood and waterproof it with tar, inside and out.   Then construct decks and stall throughout its interior. **Genesis 6:14**

Did you know that you were part of God's positive design?

God gave Noah instructions to build an ark. He gave him all the supplies he needed in order to accomplish the new design. Noah didn't know what an ark looked like, but God supplied him with his every need. He was criticized as the ark was being built, but he continued to build.

God protected and covered him while he went through the process of completion. He was given the anointing and the power, even when he couldn't picture the design visually. Then, when he was finished, God closed the doors of the ark for a reason. He couldn't take everyone with him to take part of the final product.

This is how God works. He gives you the power and anointing to build your design. He will sometimes close the door on people that didn't support you in the first place. Noah started off with a new beginning, new people, and new ideas once the storm finished. God put him in a position to start all over. So, if you start that design that He has ordained, stay focused and be mindful that in the end, a new beginning is coming your way.

Day 23 Prayer:

Father God,

Thank you for my positive design. You created me to be more than a conqueror and you gave me the power needed to build. With my design, I became a better person. I thank you for giving me the tools, the mindset, and the pathway to complete my design.

In Jesus Name,

Amen

Design is not just what it looks like and feels like.
Design is how it works.

Steve Jobs

Today's Affirmation:

_____

_____

_____

_____

_____

_____

_____

Positive Words:

_____

_____

_____

_____

_____

_____

_____

Journal your thoughts:

_____

_____

_____

_____

_____

_____

_____

Positively Courageous   Day 24

*David said to the Philistine, "You come against me with sword and spear and javelin, but I come against you in the name of the L*ORD *Almighty, the God of the armies of Israel, whom you have defied. – **1 Samuel 17:45***

David made some serious mistakes in his life. But, one thing was for sure, he was very courageous in his actions. He had a great prayer life and repented each time he fell short of the glory of God. Although he was a complete mess-up in the eyes of man, God didn't see him that way. God was looking solely at his courageous heart.

Goliath talked a lot of trash about God and David was not having it. David stood up to the giant. His brothers, along with the king, said he was too young to take down such a big giant. One thing was certain, David knew God was never going to leave him nor forsake him in battle. His faith and confidence were not in the shield, sword, or army…it was in God.

Like David, we can't be afraid of the obstacles that stand in front of us. We must be courageous in battle and be willing to be the one that God can depend on. David won the battle against the giant. He didn't win by strength or power. He believed in God and became positively courageous.

Day 24 Prayer:

Father God,

Through every trial, every test, and every battle, please make me positively courageous! Give me the strength needed to defeat the enemy each time. I say yes to your will and your way. I want to gain the courage to march forward and knock down all of the obstacles that stand in my way of greatness.

In Jesus Name,

Amen

All of our dreams can come true, if we have the courage to pursue them.

Walt Disney

Today's Affirmation:

_____

_____

_____

_____

_____

_____

_____

Positive Words:

_____

_____

_____

_____

_____

_____

Journal your thoughts:

_____

_____

_____

_____

_____

_____

Taking Positive Steps **Day 25**

Order my steps in thy word: and let not any iniquity have dominion over me.
– Psalms 119:116

As I grow older and wiser in Christ, I realize that God can turn a mess into a miracle. If we just move out of his way and allow him to do the work, it's already done. But how? We can start by taking positive steps with Christ.

We all know about the woman mentioned in the Bible that was bound and oppressed for eighteen long years. She had difficulty with making change and getting herself back on track. Her past was eating her up, but when Jesus came along, He set her free. She was no longer bound, and she allowed God to order her steps from that day forward. Satan could no longer rule in her life. (*Luke 13:13-17*)

Don't you want to be free from bondage? Don't you want the enemy to let you go? If so, allow God to order your steps. Read His word and let Him have dominion over your life.

For he took notice of his lowly servant girl, and from now on all generations will call me blessed. (Luke 1:48)

Let God take notice as you follow the road map that He has given you. He will never leave you, nor forsake you. Also, remember; never let someone who doesn't have your best interest at heart persuade you into jumping on a path that hasn't been ordained for YOU. Hear Him, seek Him, and trust Him. He will guide you to bigger and better things and blow your mind!

Day 25 Prayer:

Father God,

Thank you for your mercy and your grace. Thank you for ordering my steps and giving me the road map to success. Thank you for turning my mess into a miracle for all the world to see. I give you honor, glory, and praise.

In Jesus Name,

Amen

When God orders your steps, it will be a greater adventure than had you designed it yourself.

Letter # 37 (Creative Commons)

Today's Affirmation:

_____

_____

_____

_____

_____

_____

_____

Positive Words:

_____

_____

_____

_____

_____

_____

Journal your thoughts:

_____

_____

_____

_____

_____

_____

_____

*I can do all this through him who gives me strength. - **Philippians 4:3***

I can truly affirm that I can do all things through Christ, who strengthens me. I am bold enough to believe that God will take care of all my needs and get me into places that I have never seen or heard of. But I must stand on His promises. I can also attest that He gives me the power to rise above all my circumstances or obstacles that try to hinder me.

God has the power to raise you up, time and time again. Martha talked about Jesus having the power to raise her brother, Lazarus, up from the dead (***John 11: 21-27***). If He can do it for Lazarus, He can also do it for you. Martha had that futuristic kind of faith that God would give her brother the strength he needed to live again. He received a new life, just as Martha believed.   We can walk into our newness from the strength that we receive. The story of Lazarus shows us that all things are possible.

If you've fallen or feel you're at the end of your rope, God has the power to raise you up once again! It's a new day. Take advantage of it and allow God to give you the strength to RISE!

Day 26 Prayer:

Father God,

I believe that you have all the power I need in your hands. I have the faith to stand on your word and I believe in all that you have promised for my future. I am blessed, and I celebrate my victory over tragedy or downfalls. I will walk in my newness that you have given me, as I am assured that I will rise again.

In Jesus Name,

Amen

I trust in the Lord and he renews my strength. I will soar high like an eagle.

Isiah 40:31

Today's Affirmation:

_____

_____

_____

_____

_____

_____

_____

Positive Words:

_____

_____

_____

_____

_____

_____

_____

Journal your thoughts:

_____

_____

_____

_____

_____

_____

_____

"You are altogether beautiful, my love; there is no flaw in you".
– Songs of Solomon 4:17 NIV

We all struggle with different things that make us second-guess who we are in Him. But despite the struggle, Christ made us flawless when He died on the cross for our sins. It is written that with Christ, we are a new creation and the old creation is gone (*2 Corinthians 5:17*). Instead of sitting around full of guilt and shame due to our past mistakes, let us try to strive for holiness. (*Hebrews 12:14*)

Did you know that God's word is flawless too? Everything He said in his word, He has promised. When you need Him the most, He does his part in loving you and covering you just like He said He would. His refuge gives you peace and He will never leave you nor forsake you. If we run to Him and trust Him, we can stand still and allow Him to work on your behalf.

Day 27 Prayer:

Father God,

Thank you for loving me. Thank you for protecting me. Thank you for keeping me. Your word is flawless and true. You have made me in your image and I praise your holy name. I give you all honor and I believe in your word. I thank you for what you said you would do. I thank you for what you've already done. I also thank you for what you're about to do on my behalf. There is no one greater than you. You have all the power in your hands.

In Jesus Name,

Amen

No matter how beat up you are, no matter what you go through in life, no matter how difficult life is, the cross made you flawless.

Bart Millard

Today's Affirmation:

_____
_____
_____
_____
_____
_____
_____

Positive Words:

_____
_____
_____
_____
_____
_____
_____

Journal your thoughts:

_____
_____
_____
_____
_____
_____
_____

Positively Equipped   *Day 28*

Therefore, put on every piece of God's armor so you will be able to resist the enemy in the time of evil. Then after the battle you will be standing firm. – Ephesians 6:13

King Nebuchadnezzar, the king of Babylon, wanted three Hebrew boys by the names of Shadrach, Meshach and Abednego, to bow down to his image. The king made a ninety-foot statue and ordered everyone to bow down when they heard music being played. When the three boys refused to do so, they were threatened with being thrown in a fiery furnace. They held onto their belief of the Almighty God and would not worship anyone else, even after the threats. They didn't question their faith nor stray from their beliefs. They put on the full armor of God and stood firm during their battle with the king.

The three boys weren't sure if God had a rescue plan for their lives, but they refused to worship any other god. They were tied up and thrown in the fire. The Old Testament didn't mention Jesus by His name, but He was part of God's rescue plan. But, when they got in the fire, the king could see that they weren't tied up anymore and there was a fourth person walking around in the fire with them. *(Daniel 3:21-30)*

When they came out of the fire, the officials scanned their bodies. They had no sign of burns, their attire was intact, and there was no smell of smoke lingering on their bodies. After seeing this, the king gave an order to the officials and said no one will talk against the God they serve. Not only did the king switch up and protect them, but he also elevated the three boys to high positions in the surrounding areas. This is a prime example of three young men putting on the full armor of God.

What does God's armor consist of, you ask?

(Ephesians 6:10-18)

1) Be strong in the Lord in order to take a stand against the devil.
2) Stand your ground and believe in His word with the belt of truth.
3) Have your feet fitted with the readiness that comes from the gospel of peace.
4) Take up the shield of faith. This will extinguish all the arrows that are thrown your way.
5) Put on the helmet of salvation. Allow God to reign in your life.
6) Always have your sword of the spirit, which is the living word of God.

If you have all these components, you are fully equipped and ready for battle. The three boys believed in God, stood their ground, kept the faith, allowed God to reign in their lives, and told of God's goodness through the word that was given.

Always stay positively equipped by keeping your armor on. You will WIN!

Day 28 Prayer:

Father God,

I will keep on your armor at all times. Even when the writing is on the wall and all hope seems lost, I will trust that you will rescue me, and you will show up and show out. You have given me the equipment needed to push forward even in the fire. No weapon formed against me shall prosper.

In Jesus Name,

Amen

Nobody owes me anything. I am not at the disadvantage. I am equipped, empowered, and anointed.

Joel Osteen

Today's Affirmation:

_____

_____

_____

_____

_____

_____

_____

Positive Words:

_____

_____

_____

_____

_____

_____

_____

Journal your thoughts:

_____

_____

_____

_____

_____

_____

_____

*Let us fix our eyes on Jesus. – **Hebrews 12:2***

I've been in many races as a child. My goal was to one day be like Florence Griffith Joyner. I wasn't on her level, but I strived to be as young as the age of eight years old. I learned a lot about running back then. As a runner, one thing was for sure. When I felt defeated by the other participants, I would tend to give up, stop running, or plop down in the middle of the track.

Sometimes, the people I ran against were faster, stronger, and possibly more confident. But, halfway to the finish line in one of my races, I remember getting a surge of energy. I was determined to win the race. That was called my positive second wind.

In Hebrews, we are instructed to throw down everything that may hinder us from finishing the race. To do this, you must have the stamina and perseverance to take your run all the way to the finish line. It's easy to lose focus on the end goal, but don't be distracted by the runners that are on each side of you. All you need to do is set your eyes on the final prize.

Running a race is just like ministry. If we fix our eyes on Jesus, instead of worrying about the other runners on each side of us, we can get to God's finish line with ease. Breathe and manifest that second wind to empower you, encourage you, and motivate you to make it until the end.

With every race, it always starts out with excitement, butterflies in your stomach, and smiles going back and forth to each opponent. But, during the race, our mind may shift after looking at the power of the others around us. We may get sad, angry or bitter, because they are further along than we are. But, we must press our way through by gaining a second wind.

For me, I ran with all my strength and might. I closed my eyes for a few seconds, prayed that I would zoom past the others, and moved ahead. My second wind gave me an endurance that I didn't know I had within me. Although I didn't win the race, I still finished, feeling victorious about completing my goal. Remember, it's not where your race starts in life, it's where you finish. Pray that God will give you the strength needed to make it to the finish line and embrace your second wind.

Day 29 Prayer:

Father God,

Thank you for the second wind that gives me strength to move forward in this race. I lift my hands up in total praise to you. I will not give up and I will not give in. I will run until I reach my destiny.

In Jesus Name,

Amen

Most people never run far enough on their first wind to find out they've got a second wind.

William James

Today's Affirmation:

_____

_____

_____

_____

_____

_____

_____

Positive Words:

_____

_____

_____

_____

_____

_____

_____

Journal your thoughts:

_____

_____

_____

_____

_____

_____

_____

*Now may the Lord of peace himself give you his peace at all times and in every situation. The Lord be with you all. May the grace of our Lord Jesus Christ be with you all. — **Thessalonians 3: 16 & 18***

Wow are we already at the end of this book? What a blessing it has been to write a book, discussing *Positive Vibes Only*. Each day gave me encouragement and spoke to my spirit, in order to speak to you. I hope you are fired up and ready to go on a positive journey that will allow you to gain countless rewards. After feasting at God's table and getting the meat you needed for continuous positive nourishment, I also hope you spread positive words to others around you.

Paul gave his final words to the Thessalonians as he approached the end of his life. He knew ministering to Ephesus was going to be given to Timothy. Knowing he would be executed, Paul encouraged Timothy in his last writing, to continue teaching the gospel of Jesus Christ. He advised Timothy to move with integrity and to always give sound instruction throughout his journey.

Therefore, my brothers and sisters, after closing this book and meditating on continuous positive vibes to flow through your living vessel, remain unstoppable, unmovable, unbreakable, and always abiding in God's word. As Paul warned Timothy, stay true to what is right *(1 Timothy 4:16)*, and allow God to use you in a mighty way.

Be encouraged my friends and never look back on the negativity.

Only move forward with... *Positive Vibes Only.*

Day 30 Prayer:

Father God,

Thank you for all my many blessings. Thank you for your unconditional love towards me. Thank you for sending your angels to protect me. Thank you, thank you, and thank you again. You are worthy of all the praise.

In Jesus Name,

Amen

Positive thinking is more than just a tagline. It changes the way we behave. And I firmly believe that when I am positive, it not only makes me better, it makes those around me better.

Harvey Mackay

Today's Affirmation:

_____

_____

_____

_____

_____

_____

_____

Positive Words:

_____

_____

_____

_____

_____

_____

_____

Journal your thoughts:

_____

_____

_____

_____

_____

_____

_____

ABOUT THE AUTHOR

Teresa B. Howell

Teresa B. Howell was raised in Boston, Massachusetts. She is an educator, mentor, and advocate for students with special needs. Born and raised in the church, it was fitting to tell her story. She currently resides in Durham, North Carolina with her husband and children.

Check out her Christian Fiction novels: *That Church Life* 1, 2 & 3, available on Amazon.com and Barnesandnoble.com.

For more information or updates:
www.teresabhowell.com

www.ingramcontent.com/pod-product-compliance
Lightning Source LLC
Chambersburg PA
CBHW071601040426
42452CB00008B/1250